THESSALONIANS

HOW CAN I BE SURE?

DONALD
BAKER

10 STUDIES
FOR INDIVIDUALS
OR GROUPS

Life
Builder
Study

INTER-VARSITY PRESS
36 Causton Street, London SW1P 4ST, England
Email: ivp@ivpbooks.com
Website: www.ivpbooks.com

*Originally published in the United States of America in the LifeGuide® Bible Studies series
in 2001 by InterVarsity Press, Downers Grove, Illinois*
First published in Great Britain by Scripture Union in 2010
Second UK edition published in 2015
This edition published in Great Britain by Inter-Varsity Press 2019

British Library Cataloguing-in-Publication Data
A catalogue record for this book is available from the British Library.

ISBN: 978–1–78359–880–9

Printed in Great Britain by Ashford Colour Press Ltd, Gosport, Hampshire

*Inter-Varsity Press publishes Christian books that are true to the Bible and that communicate
the gospel, develop discipleship and strengthen the church for its mission in the world.*

*IVP originated within the Inter-Varsity Fellowship, now the Universities and Colleges Christian
Fellowship, a student movement connecting Christian Unions in universities and colleges
throughout Great Britain, and a member movement of the International Fellowship of
Evangelical Students. Website: www.uccf.org.uk. That historic association is maintained,
and all senior IVP staff and committee members subscribe to the UCCF Basis of Faith.*

Contents

Getting the Most
Out of *1 & 2 Thessalonians*

Conventional wisdom tells us that nothing is certain except death and taxes, but for most of us that is not enough. Wouldn't you like to be just as sure about where you stand with God? That's what the Thessalonians were looking for, and Paul's letters to them can help you find that assurance as well.

In the year A.D. 50, Paul entered Thessalonica while on his second missionary journey. He preached there for three weeks and was able to establish a church. However, a group of jealous Jews interpreted Paul's message to mean that he was proclaiming another ruler in opposition to the Roman emperor, and he was forced to leave town (Acts 17:1-10).

Because of Paul's concern for this young church, he sent his coworker Timothy to learn how the Thessalonians were doing. Timothy reported that the Christians' faith remained strong but that they continued to be persecuted by those who had banished Paul. Timothy also brought back questions that Paul had not had time to answer during his short stay with them.

First Thessalonians was Paul's first attempt at offering encouragement and answering questions—in fact it was probably the first of Paul's epistles. It was written from Corinth only a few months after Paul had left Thessalonica. Second Thessalonians was written a short time later to clear up misconceptions that the first letter had failed to answer.

In these letters, Paul offers encouragement in four major areas: (1) How can I be sure that I will be with Jesus after death? (2) How can I be sure that Jesus is coming again? (3) How can I be sure that Jesus hasn't forgotten me when I am suffering persecution? (4) How can I be sure that my life is pleasing to God?

Through your study of these letters, it is my hope that you will become sure of your faith and of your salvation and that, as a result, you will be able to "encourage each other with these words" (1 Thessalonians 4:18).

Suggestions for Individual Study

1. As you begin each study, pray that God will speak to you through his Word.

2. Read the introduction to the study and respond to the personal reflection question or exercise. This is designed to help you focus on God and on the theme of the study.

3. Each study deals with a particular passage—so that you can delve into the author's meaning in that context. Read and reread the passage to be studied. If you are studying a book, it will be helpful to read through the entire book prior to the first study. The questions are written using the language of the New International Version, so you may wish to use that version of the Bible. The New Revised Standard Version is also recommended.

4. This is an inductive Bible study, designed to help you discover for yourself what Scripture is saying. The study includes three types of questions. *Observation* questions ask about the basic facts: who, what, when, where and how. *Interpretation* questions delve into the meaning of the passage. *Application* questions help you discover the implications of the text for growing in Christ. These three keys unlock the treasures of Scripture.

Write your answers to the questions in the spaces provided or in a personal journal. Writing can bring clarity and deeper understanding of yourself and of God's Word.

5. It might be good to have a Bible dictionary handy. Use it to look up any unfamiliar words, names or places.

6. Use the prayer suggestion to guide you in thanking God for what you have learned and to pray about the applications that have come to mind.

7. You may want to go on to the suggestion under "Now or Later," or you may want to use that idea for your next study.

Suggestions for Members of a Group Study

1. Come to the study prepared. Follow the suggestions for individual study mentioned above. You will find that careful preparation will greatly enrich your time spent in group discussion.

2. Be willing to participate in the discussion. The leader of your group will not be lecturing. Instead, he or she will be encouraging the members of the group to discuss what they have learned. The leader will be asking the questions that are found in this guide.

3. Stick to the topic being discussed. Your answers should be based on the verses which are the focus of the discussion and not on outside authorities such as commentaries or speakers. These studies focus on a particular passage of Scripture. Only rarely should you refer to other portions of the Bible. This allows for everyone to participate in in-depth study on equal ground.

4. Be sensitive to the other members of the group. Listen attentively when they describe what they have learned. You may be surprised by their insights! Each question assumes a variety of answers. Many questions do not have "right" answers, particularly questions that aim at meaning or application. Instead the questions push us to explore the passage more thoroughly.

When possible, link what you say to the comments of others. Also, be affirming whenever you can. This will encourage some of the more hesitant members of the group to participate.

5. Be careful not to dominate the discussion. We are sometimes so eager to express our thoughts that we leave too little opportunity for others to respond. By all means participate! But allow others to also.

6. Expect God to teach you through the passage being discussed and through the other members of the group. Pray that you will have an enjoyable and profitable time together, but also that as a result of the study you will find ways that you can take action individually and/or as a group.

7. Remember that anything said in the group is considered confidential and should not be discussed outside the group unless specific permission is given to do so.

8. If you are the group leader, you will find additional suggestions at the back of the guide.

1

How Can I Be Sure of My Beliefs?

Acts 17:1-15

A college professor who was an atheist often challenged me, "Mr. Baker, sometime you have got to explain to me how anybody could possibly go through four years of college and still be a Christian!"

GROUP DISCUSSION. When have you had to defend your beliefs in front of people who disagreed? What did you say?

PERSONAL REFLECTION. What questions and doubts do you have regarding your faith? Express these to God.

Standing up for the minority is never comfortable, but when the majority happens to be an angry mob, and you are expected to be the minority spokesperson, and you aren't sure you are ready to defend what you believe, then it becomes a nightmare. In this study we will meet a man in just such a predicament. *Read Acts 17:1-15.*

---

1. What challenges and discouragements would you have faced as a Christian in Thessalonica?

2. Why was there so much anger and jealousy directed against Paul (vv. 4-5)?

3. To what extent were the accusations made against the Christians a misunderstanding?

4. How should we, as Christians, react to jealousy and misunderstanding?

5. Imagine yourself as Jason (vv. 5-7). You have been a Christian about three weeks and must defend yourself and your houseguests before the city officials. How would you have felt in this position?

What would you have said?

6. If you had been Jason, what doubts might you have had about your beliefs?

7. If you had been Paul writing a letter to the Thessalonians, what would you have wanted to say to them?

8. How did the Bereans respond to Paul's teaching (vv. 11-12)?

9. The Jews from Thessalonica make an appearance again (v. 13). How would you characterize the Bereans in comparison to the Thessalonians?

10. Sometimes Christians are accused of being close-minded. What can the Thessalonians and Bereans teach you about being open-minded?

about being confident of your beliefs?

---

11. When have you experienced doubts and discouragement similar to those of the Thessalonians?

---

12. In what ways can Christians help each other to be assured of what they believe?

Pray that God will help you to find assurance regarding the doubts and discouragements that have been expressed.

Now or Later

How would you explain your beliefs to someone who is unfamiliar with the Christian faith? Write out an outline of your basic beliefs.

2

How Can I Be Sure of My Purpose?

1 Thessalonians 1

A lighthouse has become a common analogy for a Christian group. Just as a lighthouse stands in a dark and dangerous spot, flashing its message of warning and pointing to safe harbor, a Christian community should also be a prominent and unmistakable sign to its neighbors.

GROUP DISCUSSION. What is the reputation of your church or fellowship group throughout the community?

PERSONAL REFLECTION. In what ways have you, your home and your church been like a lighthouse in the neighborhood?

How can you help your church or fellowship group become a lighthouse? This passage describes how the church in Thessalonica was able to do it. *Read 1 Thessalonians 1.*

1. What would have drawn you to want to be a part of the church in Thessalonica?

2. What facts convinced Paul that the Thessalonians' faith was genuine (v. 4)?

3. Paul writes that he remembers the Thessalonians' "work produced by faith," "labor prompted by love" and "endurance inspired by hope" (v. 3). How do you think he could tell that faith, love and hope were behind their actions?

4. Who do you know that has demonstrated this kind of faith, and how has that inspired you?

5. What role has the Holy Spirit played in the Thessalonians' faith (vv. 5-6)?

6. How has the Holy Spirit brought conviction and joy to you?

7. What role did Paul, Silas and Timothy have in the Thessalonians' conversion (v. 6)?

8. When is it wise and when is it unwise to imitate another Christian (vv. 6-7)?

9. What were the results of the Thessalonians' strong faith (vv. 8-10)?

10. How can your faith (and the faith of your church or fellowship group) become more of a witness to others?

11. How would this chapter have been an encouragement to the Thessalonians?

How is it an encouragement to you?

Pray that you, your home and your fellowship group can be effective lighthouses for God.

Now or Later

Peter wrote a beautiful description of how Christians are to bring light to their communities. *Read 1 Peter 2:4-12.* What metaphors does Peter use to describe the church, and what does each one teach you about the purpose of the church?

3

How Can I Be Sure of My Message?

1 Thessalonians 2:1-16

"Christians and non-Christians have something in common: we're both uptight about evangelism."*

GROUP DISCUSSION. Tell the group about an experience you had in either (a) telling someone about your faith or (b) having someone tell you about their faith.

PERSONAL REFLECTION. What has been positive and negative about sharing your faith with others?

For Paul, evangelism was always delightful and exciting. In this passage he tells us why talking about Christ was such a positive experience for him. *Read 1 Thessalonians 2:1-16.*

1. If you had been Paul, what excuses might you have had not to preach to the Thessalonians?

2. What attitudes enabled Paul to continue preaching despite opposition (vv. 3-6)?

3. What does this teach you about proper and improper reasons for witnessing to others?

4. How was Paul "like a mother caring for her little children" (vv. 7-9)?

5. In what specific ways can gentleness and caring become more a part of your evangelistic efforts?

6. Paul claims to have been "holy, righteous and blameless" (v. 10) among the Thessalonians. If this is important, how can imperfect people dare to do evangelism?

7. How is a father dealing with his children a good example of an evangelist (vv. 11-12)?

8. What difficulties did the Thessalonians face in sharing their faith with others (vv. 14-16)?

9. What encouragement does Paul give them not to give up?

10. In what ways have you found evangelism to be difficult?

11. What ideas and encouragement from this passage can help you overcome these difficulties?

Pray that God will give you positive experiences of sharing your faith in a caring way.

Now or Later

Pair up with another member of your group. Take turns explaining the gospel to each other as you would if the other person had never heard it before.

—————————

*Rebecca Manley Pippert, *Out of the Saltshaker,* 2nd ed. (Downers Grove, Ill.: InterVarsity Press, 1999).

4

How Can I Be Sure
That I Am Loved?

1 Thessalonians 2:17—3:13

Sometimes the places where we would most expect to find love—families, churches and fellowship groups—fail miserably in providing the love we crave.

GROUP DISCUSSION. On a scale of 1-10, how loved do you feel by members of your family? your church?

Why did you give these rankings?

PERSONAL REFLECTION. What have you contributed to the love people feel in your family? in your church?

In this study, Paul writes about a place where love will "increase and overflow for each other and for everyone else" (1 Thessalonians 3:12). *Read 1 Thessalonians 2:17—3:13.*

___

1. How would you feel if you received a personal letter like this in the mail today?

2. What evidence do you find in this passage that Paul really did love the Thessalonians?

---

3. How do you most often express your love for others?

What ideas from this passage can help you become even better at expressing love?

---

4. What fears caused Paul to send Timothy to Thessalonica (3:2-5)?

---

5. How can a person like Timothy bring reassurance to people who are struggling?

---

6. Why did Paul warn the Thessalonians that they were destined for persecution?

---

7. How can you be prepared for trials and persecutions?

8. Why was Timothy's report such good news to Paul (3:6-8)?

9. What are Paul's desires for the Thessalonians (3:10-13)?

How do these desires reflect Paul's love and caring?

10. How might Paul's example have helped the Thessalonians' love to "increase and overflow" (v. 12)?

11. How can you (as an individual or as a group member) help love to increase within your family, church or small group?

Pray for people who are feeling unloved. Pray for your ability to express love.

Now or Later

The book of James gives many practical suggestions of how love can be put into action. *Read through James,* making a list of these examples.

5

How Can I Be Sure of God's Approval?

1 Thessalonians 4:1-12

Our emotional need for approval is almost as intense as our need for love, but the two are quite different. In order to receive approval, a condition or qualification must be met. Approval must be earned and is granted because of what a person does. Approval, unlike love, has to do with "doing." God will always love us, but he may not always approve of our way of living.

GROUP DISCUSSION. Ask each member of the group to give an example of either love or approval, without revealing which they intend to illustrate. Have the group vote on which of the two their example describes.

PERSONAL REFLECTION. Think of a time when you have received approval from someone important in your life. How did that feel? What did you have to do to receive it?

Many have struggled their entire life to earn the approval of a parent or spouse and have never received it. Paul tells us that it is possible to experience God's pleasure in the way that we live. *Read 1 Thessalonians 4:1-12.*

1. Using the passage, complete the following sentence: "A person who pleases God is a person who . . ."

2. Even though Paul acknowledges that the Thessalonians are pleasing God, he urges them to "do this more and more" (v. 1). Why is it important to keep reminding each other of how we ought to live?

3. What experiences have you had of being held accountable for your lifestyle?

How have you helped to hold others accountable?

4. How does Paul define sexual immorality in this passage (vv. 3-8)?

5. What reasons does Paul give for avoiding sexual immorality?

6. How does sexual immorality "wrong" or "take advantage of" others (v. 6)?

7. What does God find pleasing and displeasing about your sexual life?

8. In verses 9 and 10 Paul commends the Thessalonians for their love. What could a group with such a reputation do to love each other even more?

How can these ideas be applied to your church or fellowship group?

9. Scholars agree that verses 11 and 12 were directed toward members of the church who had quit working and were relying on the kindness of their fellow Christians to provide them with necessities. Why would Paul have been concerned about the effect this attitude was having on outsiders?

10. What do unbelievers notice about your work habits that attracts them to Christ?

What work habits detract from your Christian witness?

---

11. Paul has given commands in this passage concerning sexual immorality, love for fellow Christians and work. What can you do this week to become more obedient in one of these areas?

Take time to confess to God the areas of your life he finds displeasing. Ask for his help in living a life that pleases him.

Now or Later

The following verses speak of people receiving God's approval. What do you learn from each verse about finding God's approval for yourself? Be sure to look at the Scripture surrounding each verse.

Romans 14:18

2 Corinthians 10:18

Galatians 1:10

1 Thessalonians 2:4

2 Timothy 2:15

6

How Can I Be Sure That Christ Is Coming Back?

1 Thessalonians 4:13—5:11

Death, thou wast once an uncouth hideous thing,
  Nothing but bones.
  The sad effect of sadder grones;
Thy mouth was open, but thou couldst not sing.

For we consider'd thee as at some six
  Or ten years hence,
  After the losse of life and sense,
Flesh being turn'd to dust, and bones to sticks.

But since our Saviours death did put some bloud
  Into thy face;
  Thou art grown fair and full of grace,
Much in request, much sought for, as a good.

George Herbert

GROUP DISCUSSION. Ask each member of the group to describe the last funeral they attended. What was the mood of that funeral? (somber? hopeless? triumphant?) Why did that mood prevail?

PERSONAL REFLECTION. What fears do you have about death?

A crisis occurred in the Thessalonian church when one of their members died. Since they had expected to all be alive when Christ returned, they were now confused. Did this mean their friend would miss out on Christ's coming? Had this person died because God was angry with them? How much longer would it be before Christ finally did return? Perhaps you have wondered about similar questions. In this passage, Paul seeks to calm our fears and encourage us to look forward to the day we meet our maker. *Read 1 Thessalonians 4:13—5:11.*

---

1. What do you find frightening about Paul's words?

What do you find comforting?

---

2. In what ways is a Christian's grief different from a nonbeliever's (4:13)?

---

3. When has grief affected your life?

What role did faith play in your grieving process?

---

4. What sequence of events does Paul say will occur when Christ returns (4:16-17)?

5. How would Paul's words have encouraged the Thessalonians?

How can they help you to face your own fears about death?

6. Why are the examples of a thief (5:2) and a woman in labor (5:3) good analogies for what will happen when Christ returns?

7. What different kinds of reactions will people have to Christ's return?

How will you react if it occurs today?

8. What dangers are associated with living in darkness (5:5-7)?

9. What instructions does Paul give for living in the light (5:8)?

10. Paul tells us that our defensive weapons against darkness are faith, love and hope (5:8). What are some practical ways in which these virtues can defend you?

11. What is God's plan for us (5:9-11)?

_____

12. How can a person prepare for "the day of the Lord"?

Thank God for the promise of Christ's return. Ask him to give you confidence regarding the future.

Now or Later

Fear and confusion struck Jesus' disciples during their last hours with him before his death. Look up the questions the disciples asked him during this troubled time in *John 13:36 and 14:5, 8.*

What problems were the disciples struggling with?

How did Jesus answer their questions?

What promises did Jesus make?

What is required of us in order to receive these promises?

7

How Can I Be Sure of God's People?

1 Thessalonians 5:12-28

Ben Patterson has the following to say about Christians: "People in the church are like porcupines in a snowstorm. We need each other to keep warm, but we prick each other if we get too close."*

GROUP DISCUSSION. Your group has been asked to develop a top-ten list for a popular late night television show. Make a list on the topic "Top 10 Rules for Getting Along with Your Friends."

PERSONAL REFLECTION. What qualities make you a good person to have as a friend?

Any group of people needs rules for getting along, and the church is no exception. Paul so wants the Thessalonians to "live in peace with each other" (1 Thessalonians 5:13) that he closes his first letter to them with several instructions on how they can do this. These are instructions that have never gone out of date and can still be used to end the quarrels, hurt feelings and resentments in your church or fellowship group. *Read 1 Thessalonians 5:12-28.*

1. What do you find compelling about the kind of community

described in these verses?

---

2. How does Paul instruct the Thessalonians to treat their Christian leaders?

---

3. What could you do to show respect for one of your hard-working leaders?

---

4. When should you speak words of warning or admonishment to a friend (v. 14)?

---

5. How can you do this and still "live in peace with each other"?

---

6. What does it mean to be joyful "always," pray "continually" and give thanks "in all circumstances" (vv. 16-18)?

7. What would help your church or fellowship group become a stronger community of prayer?

8. Verses 19-22 teach about a Christian's relationship with the Holy Spirit. How might a person treat prophecy with contempt?

9. How can you test things like prophecy or teaching to find out if they are good or evil?

10. How could a greater openness to the Spirit improve human relationships within your Christian group?

11. Look through the passage again, and pick out the actions and attitudes (stated or implied) which are displeasing to God. What are they?

12. What can you do as a group to help and encourage each other to avoid these sins?

What will God do to help (vv. 23-24)?

13. What has this passage taught you about the role of friends in helping you to live a Christian life?

Pray for the spiritual life of each of your friends and each of your Christian leaders.

Now or Later

Using verses 12 and 13 as a guide, plan an event that will honor the leaders of your church or fellowship group. Ideas might include a party, a barrage of letters, a gift or a service of encouragement and prayer.

*Ben Patterson, *Leadership* 1, no. 2, in *Bible Illustrator for Windows* ©1990-1998 by Parsons Technology.

8

How Can I Be Sure
That I Will
Go to Heaven?

Only one person in the Bible received a direct promise of heaven, and he was a thief. Still, most Christians are confident that they are going to heaven.

GROUP DISCUSSION. Divide into three groups: the powerful politicians, the wealthy entrepreneurs and the brilliant scientists. Give each group five minutes to develop an argument as to why the other groups should elect them to become immortal.

PERSONAL REFLECTION. If you were to die tonight, and God asked why he should let you into heaven, how would you answer?

Can I know for sure that I will go to heaven? This is a question that plagued the Thessalonians to such an extent that even after the comfort of his first letter, Paul has to write again and give further encouragement. It was difficult for these young Christians to believe that the suffering of their present life would really be followed by the eternal joy of heaven. Perhaps you also wonder if heaven really exists and if you can be sure of going there. If so, you will find Paul writing this passage directly to you. *Read 2 Thessalonians 1.*

---

1. What do you most admire about the Thessalonians?

---

2. Why do you think that in times of persecution, some people's faith and love grows while others' fails (v. 4)?

How can you make sure that yours is the kind that will grow?

---

3. What is the "evidence that God's judgment is right" (v. 5)?

---

4. "Suffering . . . is not to be thought of as evidence that God has forsaken us, but as evidence that God is with us."* How has God been evident in your times of suffering?

---

5. Paul proclaims that "God is just." How does he describe God's justice (vv. 6-10)?

6. How do you think suffering people like the Thessalonians would have responded to this teaching about God's justice?

7. How can God's justice encourage you when things are "just not fair"?

8. According to this passage, what makes a person "worthy of the kingdom" (v. 5) or "worthy of [God's] calling" (v. 11)?

9. What will cause God to punish some people when he returns (vv. 8-10)?

10. In light of his teaching about God's judgment, why does Paul pray as he does in verses 11-12?

11. If someone were to pray this prayer for you, what is one specific way in which you would want God to change your life?

Use verses 11 and 12 as your prayer, replacing the words you *and* your *with the names of each member of your group.*

Now or Later

In the book of Matthew, Jesus has much to say about who will enter heaven and who will be excluded. What does each of these passages teach about entering heaven?

Matthew 5:19-20

Matthew 7:21

Matthew 8:10-12

Matthew 18:1-9

Matthew 19:23-30

Matthew 23:13

---

*Leon Morris, *The First and Second Epistles to the Thessalonians,* New International Commentary on the New Testament (Grand Rapids, Mich.: Eerdmans, 1959), p. 198.

9

How Can I Be Sure of God's Power?

2 Thessalonians 2

The LORD is my rock, my fortress and my deliverer;
my God is my rock in whom I take refuge.
He is my shield and the horn of my salvation, my stronghold.
(Psalm 18:2)

GROUP DISCUSSION. Rank the following threats to world safety in order of their severity, with number one being the most crucial problem.

___ pollution of the environment
___ weapons buildup
___ political unrest
___ crime
___ poverty
___ depletion of resources
___ epidemics
___ natural disasters
___ other

Why did you rank these threats as you did?

PERSONAL REFLECTION. What do you worry about? Talk to God about your fears.

How will the world end? Will there be nuclear war? an evil empire? the destruction of civilization? Paul advises us that Satan has yet to attack us with the worst he has, and when he does, it will be a fearful time to be alive. However, Paul also promises that God will always be in control. *Read 2 Thessalonians 2.*

---

1. How do you feel about the future after reading this passage?

---

2. In 1 Thessalonians 4:13-18 we saw how Paul responded to the fears of the Thessalonians that if they died before Christ returned, they would miss the joy Christ had for them. Apparently, after Paul sent the first letter, someone tried to convince the Thessalonians that the day of the Lord had already come. Considering the misconceptions they already had about Christ's return, how would this have affected them?

---

3. What is Paul's proof that the day of the Lord has not come (vv. 3, 9)?

---

4. What can you learn about the "man of lawlessness" from this passage (vv. 3-4, 7-10)?

---

5. Paul reminds the Thessalonians that he has already told them what is holding back the lawless one (vv. 5-6). Unfortunately, this was something he told them orally, and we don't know what he said.

Despite the fact that this information is missing, what can be learned about the way God prevents his people from being destroyed?

---

6. In what ways have you noticed the "secret power of lawlessness" (v. 7) to be already at work?

---

7. Why will God cause people to believe the lies of the lawless one (v. 11)?

---

8. What contrasts do you find between those that God condemns (vv. 10-12) and those that he chooses for salvation (vv. 13-17)?

---

9. How can you be sure that you are a part of the group chosen for salvation?

---

10. Even for Christians, the lawless one will bring fear and testing. What can you do to prepare yourself to withstand him?

What is God doing to strengthen you?

11. How can this passage encourage you about facing the future?

Pray for the strength to trust God through the hard times to come.

Now or Later

Read more about the day of the Lord in Matthew 24.

What signs will warn us that the day of the Lord is coming?

What difficulties will God's people face?

How will God's power be displayed?

What can you be doing now to prepare for the day of the Lord?

10

How Can I Be Sure That I Am Doing My Part?

2 Thessalonians 3

Christian leaders sometimes speak of the "twenty, eighty principle" to indicate that twenty percent of the people do eighty percent of the work and giving.

GROUP DISCUSSION. What excuses can you think of for why a person might choose to be a part of the eighty percent that does only twenty percent of the work?

PERSONAL REFLECTION. Are you a part of the twenty percent or the eighty percent? Why?

Members of the Thessalonian church were refusing to take responsibility. Some had quit working because they thought Jesus would be back any moment and didn't see any reason to exert themselves. Others relaxed because there were plenty of wealthier members in the church who were always willing to share. Regardless of the reason, Paul was abhorred by such laziness and set the rule, "If a man will not work, he shall not eat." *Read 2 Thessalonians 3.*

1. Which of the following modern situations seems most similar to the one Paul describes in these verses? Why?

a. A homeless person begging for spare change. b. An adult child who has moved back to live with Mom and Dad in order to cut back on expenses. c. A coworker who consistently shirks his or her responsibility on joint projects. d. A person who regularly refuses to teach a class or lead a Bible study, even though well qualified. e. A friend who has never picked up the check.

2. What work does Paul expect every one of his readers to perform (vv. 1-5)?

3. What do you learn from these verses about the work and responsibility of prayer?

4. What encouragement and ideas do these verses give you concerning your own prayer life?

5. What problems do you imagine the idle brothers were causing for the rest of the church and community?

6. In what ways do lazy Christians still continue to take advantage of the work of others? What are the effects?

7. How did Paul make himself an example of the proper attitude toward work (vv. 7-9)?

8. How can you become a similar example to others?

9. What actions are to be taken against those who refuse to work (vv. 12-15)?

10. Why would this have been a good method of dealing with the problem in Thessalonica?

11. What principles for discipline of Christians do you find in this passage?

Pray for a positive attitude toward your work, and pray for those who work the hardest in your church or group.

Now or Later

Review what you have learned in your study of Thessalonians.

12. Paul speaks about the second coming of Christ in both 1 Thessalonians 4:13—5:11 and 2 Thessalonians 2. How would you summarize his teaching?

_____

13. What effect should knowledge about the second coming have on our daily living?

_____

14. What principles have you learned about enduring times of suffering (1 Thessalonians 1:2-7; 3:1-10)?

about sharing your faith with others (1 Thessalonians 2)?

about pleasing God (1 Thessalonians 4:1-12; 5:12-22; 2 Thessalonians 3:6-15)?

about God's justice (2 Thessalonians 1:3-10)?

_____

15. What changes have you observed in your life as a result of studying Thessalonians?

Leader's Notes

Leading a Bible discussion can be an enjoyable and rewarding experience. But it can also be *scary*—especially if you've never done it before. If this is your feeling, you're in good company. When God asked Moses to lead the Israelites out of Egypt, he replied, "O Lord, please send someone else to do it!" (Ex 4:13). It was the same with Solomon, Jeremiah and Timothy, but God helped these people in spite of their weaknesses, and he will help you as well.

You don't need to be an expert on the Bible or a trained teacher to lead a Bible discussion. The idea behind these inductive studies is that the leader guides group members to discover for themselves what the Bible has to say. This method of learning will allow group members to remember much more of what is said than a lecture would.

These studies are designed to be led easily. As a matter of fact, the flow of questions through the passage from observation to interpretation to application is so natural that you may feel that the studies lead themselves. This study guide is also flexible. You can use it with a variety of groups—student, professional, neighborhood or church groups. Each study takes forty-five to sixty minutes in a group setting.

There are some important facts to know about group dynamics and encouraging discussion. The suggestions listed below should enable you to effectively and enjoyably fulfill your role as leader.

Preparing for the Study

1. Ask God to help you understand and apply the passage in your own life. Unless this happens, you will not be prepared to lead others. Pray too for the various members of the group. Ask God to open your hearts to the message of his Word and motivate you to action.

2. Read the introduction to the entire guide to get an overview of the entire book and the issues which will be explored.

3. As you begin each study, read and reread the assigned Bible passage to familiarize yourself with it.

4. This study guide is based on the New International Version of the Bible.

It will help you and the group if you use this translation as the basis for your study and discussion.

5. Carefully work through each question in the study. Spend time in meditation and reflection as you consider how to respond.

6. Write your thoughts and responses in the space provided in the study guide. This will help you to express your understanding of the passage clearly.

7. It might help to have a Bible dictionary handy. Use it to look up any unfamiliar words, names or places. (For additional help on how to study a passage, see chapter five of *How to Lead a LifeBuilder Study*, IVP, 2018.)

8. Consider how you can apply the Scripture to your life. Remember that the group will follow your lead in responding to the studies. They will not go any deeper than you do.

9. Once you have finished your own study of the passage, familiarize yourself with the leader's notes for the study you are leading. These are designed to help you in several ways. First, they tell you the purpose the study guide author had in mind when writing the study. Take time to think through how the study questions work together to accomplish that purpose. Second, the notes provide you with additional background information or suggestions on group dynamics for various questions. This information can be useful when people have difficulty understanding or answering a question. Third, the leader's notes can alert you to potential problems you may encounter during the study.

10. If you wish to remind yourself of anything mentioned in the leader's notes, make a note to yourself below that question in the study.

Leading the Study

1. Begin the study on time. Open with prayer, asking God to help the group to understand and apply the passage.

2. Be sure that everyone in your group has a study guide. Encourage the group to prepare beforehand for each discussion by reading the introduction to the guide and by working through the questions in the study.

3. At the beginning of your first time together, explain that these studies are meant to be discussions, not lectures. Encourage the members of the group to participate. However, do not put pressure on those who may be hesitant to speak during the first few sessions. You may want to suggest the following guidelines to your group.

☐ Stick to the topic being discussed.

☐ Your responses should be based on the verses which are the focus of the discussion and not on outside authorities such as commentaries or speakers.

☐ These studies focus on a particular passage of Scripture. Only rarely should you refer to other portions of the Bible. This allows for everyone to participate in in-depth study on equal ground.

☐ Anything said in the group is considered confidential and will not be discussed outside the group unless specific permission is given to do so.

☐ We will listen attentively to each other and provide time for each person present to talk.

☐ We will pray for each other.

4. Have a group member read the introduction at the beginning of the discussion.

5. Every session begins with a group discussion question. The question or activity is meant to be used before the passage is read. The question introduces the theme of the study and encourages group members to begin to open up. Encourage as many members as possible to participate, and be ready to get the discussion going with your own response.

This section is designed to reveal where our thoughts or feelings need to be transformed by Scripture. That is why it is especially important not to read the passage before the discussion question is asked. The passage will tend to color the honest reactions people would otherwise give because they are, of course, supposed to think the way the Bible does.

You may want to supplement the group discussion question with an ice-breaker to help people to get comfortable. See the community section of the *Small Group Starter Kit* (IVP, 1995) for more ideas.

You also might want to use the personal reflection question with your group. Either allow a time of silence for people to respond individually or discuss it together.

6. Have a group member (or members if the passage is long) read aloud the passage to be studied. Then give people several minutes to read the passage again silently so that they can take it all in.

7. Question 1 will generally be an overview question designed to briefly survey the passage. Encourage the group to look at the whole passage, but try to avoid getting sidetracked by questions or issues that will be addressed later in the study.

8. As you ask the questions, keep in mind that they are designed to be used just as they are written. You may simply read them aloud. Or you may prefer to express them in your own words.

There may be times when it is appropriate to deviate from the study guide. For example, a question may have already been answered. If so, move on to the next question. Or someone may raise an important question not covered in the guide. Take time to discuss it, but try to keep the group from going off on tangents.

9. Avoid answering your own questions. If necessary, repeat or rephrase them until they are clearly understood. Or point out something you read in the leader's notes to clarify the context or meaning. An eager group quickly becomes passive and silent if they think the leader will do most of the talking.

10. Don't be afraid of silence. People may need time to think about the question before formulating their answers.

11. Don't be content with just one answer. Ask, "What do the rest of you think?" or "Anything else?" until several people have given answers to the question.

12. Acknowledge all contributions. Try to be affirming whenever possible. Never reject an answer. If it is clearly off-base, ask, "Which verse led you to that conclusion?" or again, "What do the rest of you think?"

13. Don't expect every answer to be addressed to you, even though this will probably happen at first. As group members become more at ease, they will begin to truly interact with each other. This is one sign of healthy discussion.

14. Don't be afraid of controversy. It can be very stimulating. If you don't resolve an issue completely, don't be frustrated. Move on and keep it in mind for later. A subsequent study may solve the problem.

15. Periodically summarize what the group has said about the passage. This helps to draw together the various ideas mentioned and gives continuity to the study. But don't preach.

16. At the end of the Bible discussion you may want to allow group members a time of quiet to work on an idea under "Now or Later." Then discuss what you experienced. Or you may want to encourage group members to work on these ideas between meetings. Give an opportunity during the session for people to talk about what they are learning.

17. Conclude your time together with conversational prayer, adapting the prayer suggestion at the end of the study to your group. Ask for God's help in following through on the commitments you've made.

18. End on time.

Many more suggestions and helps are found in *How to Lead a LifeBuilder Study.*

Components of Small Groups

A healthy small group should do more than study the Bible. There are four components to consider as you structure your time together.

Nurture. Small groups help us to grow in our knowledge and love of God. Bible study is the key to making this happen and is the foundation of your small group.

Community. Small groups are a great place to develop deep friendships with other Christians. Allow time for informal interaction before and after each study. Plan activities and games that will help you get to know each other. Spend time having fun together—going on a picnic or cooking dinner together.

Worship and prayer. Your study will be enhanced by spending time praising God together in prayer or song. Pray for each other's needs—and keep track of how God is answering prayer in your group. Ask God to help you to apply what you are learning in your study.

Outreach. Reaching out to others can be a practical way of applying what you are learning, and it will keep your group from becoming self-focused. Host a series of evangelistic discussions for your friends or neighbors. Clean up the yard of an elderly friend. Serve at a soup kitchen together, or spend a day working in the community.

Many more suggestions and helps in each of these areas are found in the *Small Group Starter Kit.* You will also find information on building a small group. Reading through the starter kit will be worth your time.

Study 1. Acts 17:1-15. How Can I Be Sure of My Beliefs?

Purpose: To provide encouragement to your group in facing challenges for which they do not feel prepared.

Question 2. It was Paul's regular practice upon entering a new city to go to the synagogue and preach. Here he was able to convince some Jewish listeners to follow Christ. However, the majority of his converts were Gentiles who worshiped in the synagogue and believed in God. Among these were a number of highly respected women—probably wives of the principal citizens. It would have been very natural for the Jews to fear that they were losing influence over these people and so resent Paul for "stealing" them.

Question 3. Paul and Silas were being accused of the serious crime of high treason for causing a radical social upheaval. One of the reasons that Acts was written was to demonstrate that the Christians were good citizens. Although they called Christ their king and refused to worship Caesar, this didn't mean that they were trying to overthrow the government. There did seem to be trouble (and even riots) wherever Paul preached, but Paul wasn't the one inciting these uprisings.

Question 4. Paul reacted by boldly continuing to proclaim the message without compromise. He did, however, obey the agreement to leave town, which he made with the city officials. Paul also avoided trouble by leaving town immediately when the troublemakers came to Berea (v. 14).

Question 7. This question, along with question 11, can build the group's expectations for what they will find in 1 and 2 Thessalonians. Be sensitive to members who are ready to express a need that they hope this study will answer.

Questions 8-9. "Luke obviously admires their enthusiasm for Paul's preaching, together with their industry and unprejudiced openness in studying the Scriptures. They combined receptivity with critical questioning. The verb for 'examine' *(anakrino)* is used of judicial investigations. . . . It implies integrity and absence of bias. Ever since then, the adjective 'Berean' has been applied to people who study the Scriptures with impartiality and care" (John Stott, *The Message of Acts* [Downers Grove, Ill.: InterVarsity Press, 1990], p. 274).

Question 10. "In Thessalonica Paul 'reasoned', 'explained', 'proved', 'proclaimed' and 'persuaded', while in Berea the Jews eagerly 'received' the message and diligently 'examined' the Scriptures. It was inevitable in Jewish evangelism that the Old Testament Scriptures should be both the textbook and the court of appeal. What is impressive is that neither speaker nor hearers used Scripture in a superficial, unintelligent or proof-texting way. On the contrary, Paul 'argued' out of the Scriptures and the Bereans 'examined' them to see if his arguments were cogent. And we may be sure that Paul welcomed and encouraged this thoughtful response. He believed in doctrine (his message has theological content), but not in indoctrination (tyrannical instruction demanding uncritical acceptance). . . . Paul's arguments and his hearers' studies went hand in hand. I do not doubt that he also bathed both in prayer, asking the Holy Spirit of truth to open his mouth to explain, and his hearers' minds to grasp, the good news of salvation in Christ" (Stott, *Message of Acts*, pp. 274-75).

Study 2. 1 Thessalonians 1. How Can I Be Sure of My Purpose?

Purpose: To help group members find ways in which their faith can impact others.

Question 2. Who God has chosen is essentially a secret known to him alone. "So how could the missionaries possibly dare to claim that they knew it? They tell us. They give two bases for their knowledge, the first in the following verse (5), relating to their evangelism, and the second in the previous verse (3), relating to the Thessalonians' holiness. Both were evidences of the activities of the Holy Spirit, first in the missionaries (giving power to their preaching) and secondly in the converts (producing in them faith, love and hope), and therefore of the election of the Thessalonians. This shows that the doctrine of election, far from making evangelism unnecessary, makes it indispensable. For it is only through the preaching and receiving of the gospel that God's secret purpose comes to be revealed and known" (John Stott, *The Gospel and the End of Time* [Downers Grove, Ill.: InterVarsity Press, 1991], pp. 31-32).

Question 3. Perhaps the following definitions will help your group understand what Paul saw: *Faith* is a trust in God, which shows itself in obedient commitment. *Love* is unselfish care for someone. "Labor of love" expresses the cost of their love, not its result. *Hope* is an active constancy in the face of difficulties.

Question 5. It is noteworthy that in the same sentence Paul can speak of both the Thessalonians' suffering and joy (v. 6). Although this church faced opposition from the very beginning, the Holy Spirit filled it with a serenity that the world could neither give nor take away.

Question 7. It will probably be helpful to quickly review the activities of Paul, Silas and Timothy from study one. Paul is asking the Thessalonians to imitate the way in which he imitates Christ.

Question 8. Leon Morris comments:

> The missionary must show the new way in his life as well as in his words. His converts will begin by imitating him and go on to imitate his Master. Paul has no hesitation in saying to the Corinthians, "I beseech you therefore, be ye imitators of me" (1 Cor. 4:16), and again, "Be ye imitators of me, even as I also am of Christ" (1 Cor. 11:1). The great example for Christians is that of Christ. If they imitate their teachers it is in order that they may be brought to imitate Him more closely thereby. (*The First and Second Epistles to the Thessalonians* [Grand Rapids, Mich.: Eerdmans, 1959], p. 58)

Question 9. Your group will probably notice that the Thessalonians' faith became the talk of Macedonia and Achaia. What they may not notice at first is that their faith also caused them to "wait for his [God's] Son from heaven" (v. 10). The point is that the present behavior of the Thessalonians was determined by their firm expectation of what would happen in the future.

Question 11. You may need to remind your group of what you learned about the Thessalonian church in the last study.

Study 3. 1 Thessalonians 2:1-16. How Can I Be Sure of My Message?

Purpose: To encourage group members to share their faith with others.

Question 1. Here's some general background from John Stott:

> The brief mission in Thessalonica had been brought to an ignominious end. The public riot and the legal charges against the missionaries were so serious that they were persuaded to make a humiliating night flight from the city. Paul's critics took full advantage of his sudden disappearance. In order to undermine his authority and his gospel, they determined to discredit him. So they

launched a malicious smear campaign. By studying Paul's self-defense, it is possible for us to reconstruct their slanders. "He ran away", they sneered, "and hasn't been seen or heard of since. Obviously he's insincere, impelled by the basest motives. He's just one more of those many phony teachers who tramp up and down the Egnatian Way. In a word, he's a charlatan. He's in his job only for what he can get out of it in terms of sex, money, prestige or power. So when opposition arose, and he found himself in personal danger, he took to his heels and ran! He doesn't care about you Thessalonian disciples of his; he has abandoned you! He's much more concerned about his own skin than your welfare." (Stott, *Gospel and the End of Time*, pp. 45-46)

Question 2. "We speak, therefore, writes Paul, as men who are tested by God, approved by God, trusted by God and are seeking to please God. No secret of Christian ministry is more important than its fundamental God-centredness. The stewards of the gospel are primarily responsible neither to the church, nor to its synods or leaders, but to God himself" (Stott, *Gospel and the End of Time*, p. 50).

Question 4. Paul's concern for these people goes beyond ordinary interest. It included spiritual feeding, delight in their growth, twenty-four hour availability and the willingness to bear hardship for them.

Question 6. The Thessalonian church was apparently hearing real accusations that Paul was only trying to fleece the public. In response, Paul asks the people to look at his record. Although none of us is perfect (not even Paul), we must at least be sure that we are not using people or preaching one thing while living another.

Question 7. "Paul speaks of being like a father to his converts, no doubt in the sense that he was responsible for bringing them to spiritual birth. A father can hope that his children will follow his example, but he also has the responsibility of teaching them how to live, and he does this in a spirit of love and concern for their welfare" (I. Howard Marshall, *1 and 2 Thessalonians* [Grand Rapids, Mich.: Eerdmans, 1983], p. 74).

Question 8. We do not know the exact details of the suffering that Christians faced in Judea, but they must have been well known throughout the Christian church. We do know that in Judea Jesus was crucified, Stephen was stoned (Acts 7), and a persecution forced Christians to scatter (Acts 8).

Question 9. He encourages them by again assuring them of the truth of their message, by reminding them of others who have gone through the same difficulties and by prophesying the eventual end of their antagonists.

Study 4. 1 Thessalonians 2:17—3:13. How Can I Be Sure That I Am Loved?
Purpose: To help group members find opportunities to show love through

their church or fellowship group.

Group discussion. You could also ask people how loved they feel by the Bible study group. It might draw out positive feelings and discussion of any hurts that exist. However, depending on the makeup of your group, it might also be painful or threatening.

Question 2. This section of the letter was written to answer critics who questioned Paul's motives and conduct during his visit to Thessalonica. They claimed he had either abandoned or forgotten the Thessalonians. Paul defends himself by explaining that he had left them with great reluctance (2:17), made repeated efforts to return to them (2:17-20), sent Timothy to them (3:1-5), been overjoyed by Timothy's good news (3:6-10) and prayed for them constantly (3:11-13).

Question 4. "Paul seems to have in mind the possibility that, while the Thessalonians were in the midst of their troubles, some of their enemies, by fair words, should turn them out of the right way. Perhaps while the Gentiles were persecuting them the Jews spoke kindly to them (or Paul feared that they would) with a view to persuading them to accept Judaism, which, of course, could have as one of its effects immediate cessation of persecution" (Morris, *First and Second Epistles*, p. 101).

Question 5. "Timothy had been sent on both a nurturing and a fact-finding mission. His brief had been to stabilize the Thessalonians in their faith, to remind them that suffering for Christ was unavoidable, and to come back with news of how they were doing" (Stott, *Gospel and the End of Time*, p. 65).

Question 6. "If a person knows that something unpleasant is part of his destiny, something that is inevitable, then he will brace himself to meet it and will not think that it is a sign that he is on the wrong track or be taken by surprise by it. The belief that the Christian way inevitably involves suffering and persecution was common New Testament teaching, by both Jesus and the apostles. It was seen as part of the increasing evil in the world which would precede the parousia and the winding up of history. Christians could regard suffering with Christ as the essential preliminary to sharing in his heavenly reign, and indeed the fact of suffering as a Christian was some guarantee that one was truly a member of God's people and destined for heavenly glory. Understood in this way, tribulation should not put faith in danger, but rather strengthen it" (Marshall, *1 and 2 Thessalonians*, p. 92).

Question 8. "The thing that really rejoiced him, the thing that really strengthened him, the thing that gave him life, was the fact so clearly demonstrated by Timothy's mission, that the Thessalonians did indeed believe. Their lives were characterized by faith. This meant that they had a place in God's kingdom, and this in turn that Paul's work among them had not been in vain" (Morris, *First and Second Epistles,* p. 107).

Question 9. Paul is concerned to "supply what is lacking" (v. 10) in the Thessalonians' faith. He is not reproaching them for this lack, but encouraging them to keep making progress. The lack was probably due both to the people's slowness in spiritual growth and incomplete instruction. In particular, Paul prays that the Thessalonians will grow in love (v. 12) and holiness (v. 13).

Question 10. "[Paul] lays bare his heart of love for them. He had left them only with the greatest reluctance, and had in fact been torn away from them against his will. He had then tried hard to visit them, but all his attempts had been thwarted. Waiting for news of them, he had found the suspense unbearable and so, though at great personal cost, he had sent Timothy to encourage them and find out how they were. When Timothy came back with good news, he was over the moon with joy and thanksgiving. And all the time he had been pouring out his heart for them in prayer. The fact is that his life was inextricably bound up with theirs. 'For now we really live', he wrote, 'since you are standing firm in the Lord' (3:8)" (Stott, *Gospel and the End of Time,* p. 69).

Study 5. 1 Thessalonians 4:1-12. How Can I Be Sure of God's Approval?

Purpose: To show group members how they can please God through sexual purity, brotherly love and honest labor.

Question 1. "The whole Christian life is God-centered. The Christian does not 'walk' with a view to obtaining the maximum amount of satisfaction for himself, but in order to please his Lord. Paul does not specify any particular matter in which they should 'please' God; he is concerned with the whole bent of life" (Morris, *First and Second Epistles,* p. 118).

Question 2. God's work of perfecting us will never be complete as long as we live. It should also be noted that the first-century Greeks lived in a culture that was tolerant of many evils. For example, it was taken for granted that men would have premarital and extramarital affairs. Since the Christians had come from this culture and still lived among it, temptation was a problem they constantly fought.

Question 4. Paul was writing to contrast the Christian way of life with the promiscuity of the Greco-Roman world. F. F. Bruce sums up the situation:

> A man might have a mistress who could provide him also with intellectual companionship; the institution of slavery made it easy for him to have a concubine, while casual gratification was readily available from a harlot. The function of his wife was to manage his household and to be the mother of his legitimate children and heirs. (*1 & 2 Thessalonians,* Word Biblical Commentary [Waco, Tex.: Word, 1982], p. 82)

Question 5. Paul tells us that God will punish sexual sin (v. 6); that God has a higher, holy calling in mind for us (v. 7); and that impurity is a rejection of the Holy Spirit's leading in our lives (v. 8).

Question 6. "All sexual looseness represents an act of injustice to someone other than the two parties concerned. Adultery is an obvious violation of the rights of another. But promiscuity before marriage represents the robbing of the other of the virginity which ought to be brought to a marriage. The future partner of such a one has been defrauded" (Morris, *First and Second Epistles*, p. 126).

Question 8. "He makes their well-known love for one another the basis of an appeal that they would go on to ever new heights of love. When he later wrote 2 Corinthians he praised the practical expression of their love in making a substantial gift for the poor saints in Jerusalem (2 Cor. 8:1ff.). It is this kind of thing he has in mind here also. The passage in 2 Corinthians may indicate how well his remarks were heeded" (Morris, *First and Second Epistles*, p. 130).

Question 9. Evidently, this was a continuing problem because Paul addresses it again in 2 Thessalonians 3:6-12. What probably happened is that some members of the church believed that since Jesus would soon be returning, there was no point in working or providing for the future.

Study 6. 1 Thessalonians 4:13—5:11. How Can I Be Sure That Christ Is Coming Back?

Purpose: To answer fears that group members might have concerning Christ's coming and to help them prepare for it.

Question 2. John Stott has the following to say:

> We observe that Paul does not forbid us to grieve altogether. Mourning is natural, even for a while emotionally necessary. It would be very unnatural, indeed inhuman, not to mourn when we lose somebody near and dear to us. To be sure, it is appropriate at Christian funerals joyfully to celebrate Christ's decisive victory over death, but we do so only through tears of personal sorrow. If Jesus wept at the graveside of his beloved friend Lazarus, his disciples are surely at liberty to do the same. What Paul prohibits is not grief but hopeless grief, not all mourning but mourning *like the rest of men, who have no hope,* that is, like the pagans of his day." (*Gospel and the End of Time*, p. 94)

Question 4. In verse 15, Paul states that this sequence of events is "according to the Lord's own word." Unfortunately, we have no account of Christ saying anything like this. Probably Paul is referring to an oral teaching of Christ that was not recorded in the Gospels.

Someone may ask, "If the dead in Christ will rise on the last day, where are they now?" As soon as we die, our spirits join Christ in heaven. However, it is not until the resurrection on the last day that spirits and bodies are reunited.

Question 5. "Words can and do comfort, if they are true and gentle, and if they are spoken at the right time. In the case of the Thessalonians, to compensate for their ignorance (13), Paul taught them the great truths of the return of the Lord, the resurrection of the Christian dead, the rapture of the Christian living and the reunion of all three with each other. With these words they could indeed comfort one another" (Stott, *Gospel and the End of Time*, p. 107).

Question 6. "A thief in the night" expresses the unexpectedness of the event as well as an element of unwelcomeness for those who are not prepared. "Labor pains" is used in the Bible to "express the sheer pain and agony of unpleasant experiences" (Marshall, *1 and 2 Thessalonians*, pp. 133-34).

Question 7. "Unpredictable events have different effects on those who are unprepared for them and those who are ready for them. Paul wants to assure his readers that they are ready for the parousia, whenever it may happen" (Marshall, *1 and 2 Thessalonians*, p. 136).

Question 8. Verses 6 and 7 point out that there are certain kinds of behavior that are appropriate for the sons of night but not for the Christian. The kind of sleep that Paul is talking about here is a moral sleep in which a person is spiritually unconscious to God. Very possibly he was also speaking of a spiritual drunkenness as well. I. Howard Marshall writes, "Paul would have regarded literal sobriety as an essential aspect of the Christian life but probably this idea is contained within the more general one of a spiritual sobriety which avoids any kind of excess that would stifle sensitivity to God's revelation and purpose" (*1 and 2 Thessalonians*, p. 137).

Question 9. "We Christians are characterized by light. Therefore we can have nothing to do with the deeds of darkness. We look for the day of the Lord. Therefore we must not be caught up in this world's night. ['Self-controlled'] is the same verb as that used in v. 6 and it has a similar meaning of general temperateness, with the avoidance of all kinds of excess. It is given point here by the reference to drunkenness in the intervening verse" (Morris, *First and Second Epistles*, p. 158).

Question 10. An example might be that if we are actively showing love to others, then we will not be tempted to indulge ourselves. If I keep reminding myself of my hope of Christ's return, then I will not be surprised by it.

Study 7. 1 Thessalonians 5:12-28. How Can I Be Sure of God's People?

Purpose: To help your group understand its responsibilities toward other members of the body of Christ.

Question 2. Leon Morris comments as follows:

> He wants them to be loved, and not thought of simply as the cold voice of authority. Love is the characteristic Christian attitude to man, and this should be shown within the church. Especially is this so in relationships like those between the rulers and the ruled, which in other groups of men are apt to be formal and distant. Christian love, *agape*, is not a matter of personal liking, and it is in keeping with this that Paul expressly says that they are to esteem their rulers in love "for their work's sake." It is not a matter of personalities. It is the good of the church that is the important thing. The church cannot be expected to do its work effectively if the leaders are not being loyally supported by their fellows. It is a matter of fact that we are often slow to realize to this day that effective leadership in the church of Christ demands effective following. If we are continually critical of them that are set over us, small wonder if they are unable to perform the miracles that we demand of them. If we bear in mind "the work's sake" we may be more inclined to esteem them very highly in love. (*First and Second Epistles*, p. 167)

Questions 4-5. "The verb for help (*antechomai*) presents a graphic picture of the support which the weak needed. It is as if Paul wrote to the stronger Christians: 'Hold on to them', 'cling to them', even 'put your arm round' them. . . . One might say that the idle, the anxious and the weak were the 'problem children' of the church family, plagued respectively with problems of understanding, faith and conduct. Every church has members of this kind. We have no excuse for becoming impatient with them on the ground that they are difficult, demanding, disappointing, argumentative or rude. On the contrary, we are to be patient with all of them" (Stott, *Gospel and the End of Time*, p. 122).

Question 6. Leon Morris draws out our dependence on God:

> The Christian man is ever conscious of his dependence on God. He realizes that he is always surrounded by God's love, and that, therefore, although he is not able to achieve anything worthwhile in his own strength, he has all that he needs. This knowledge will keep him always rejoicing. Why should he be otherwise? And it will keep him always in the spirit of prayer. Prayer and rejoicing are closely related, for often the believer finds in prayer the means of removing that which was the barrier to his joy. Prayer is not to be thought of only as the offering of petitions in set words. Prayer is fellowship with God. Prayer is the realization of the presence of our Father. Though it is quite impossible for us always to be uttering the words of prayer it is possible and necessary that we should always be living in the spirit of prayer. (*First and Second Epistles*, p. 173)

Question 8. The Bible speaks of various gifts of the Spirit (Rom 12:6-8; 1 Cor 12:7-11, 28-30), which have been given for the purpose of building up the church. If a congregation is hostile or indifferent toward any of these gifts, then their practice will indeed be quenched because those who could exercise them will be reticent to do so. Paul lays particular emphasis here on the gift of prophecy, which can be defined as "speaking words of encouragement which come from God." Because of their situation, the Thessalonians would have been most in need of this gift, but perhaps they were not open to receiving it.

Question 9. Although discernment is a spiritual gift, we are given tests that all Christians can apply to a teaching: (1) Does it agree with Scripture? (2) Does it acknowledge Jesus as the Christ, sent from God? (3) Does it uphold the gospel of God's free and saving grace through Christ? (4) What is the known character of the speaker? (5) Does it build up and benefit the church?

Question 12. "The essential idea in sanctification is that of being set apart for God, but there is also the thought of the character involved in such separation. In this place Paul has both aspects in mind. Moreover, while there is a human element, in that a man must yield himself up to God, yet the primary thing is the power of God which enables this to be made good. Thus Paul's prayer is that God will bring about this sanctification" (Morris, *First and Second Epistles*, p. 180).

Study 8. 2 Thessalonians 1. How Can I Be Sure That I Will Go to Heaven?

Purpose: To assure group members that in the end, God's justice will prevail, and faithfulness will be worth the cost.

Question 2. Whether persecution causes Christians to grow or fail has much to do with their attitudes toward it. Paul is famous for seeing even shipwrecks and prison sentences as opportunities for serving Christ. Another person experiencing the same circumstances might instead accuse God of abandoning them.

Question 3. Because of the sentence structure, it is not clear whether the evidence, which Paul sees, is the suffering itself or the way in which the Thessalonians have handled themselves while suffering. What must be noted, however, is that Paul did not think of suffering as something to be avoided. In fact, he believed it to be inevitable for all Christians (1 Thess 3:3). To Paul, suffering was a means God used to teach valuable lessons. So when Paul saw that the Thessalonians were suffering and were learning from that suffering, he knew that God was working.

Question 5. In discussing this question, you may be asked how a loving God could be so vengeful. I. Howard Marshall gives this answer:

> From v. 8 it is clear that the punishment described here is for those who reject the gospel, and the content of the gospel is that "God shows his love for us in that while we were yet sinners Christ died for us" and that "while we were enemies we were reconciled to God by the death of his Son" (Rom. 5:8, 10). The God whom Paul is describing is a God who does offer love and reconciliation to his enemies, but if they refuse this offer and continue in opposition to his goodness and love, then it would seem inevitable that, having refused mercy, they must face justice. Nothing in the New Testament suggests that God's love is indifferent to justice, and that he bestows a free pardon on his enemies at the cost of failing to defend the persecuted against the persecutors. Indeed, it is difficult to see how the ultimate justice of God to those who suffer can be defended in a situation where the persecutor knows that in the end he will be freely forgiven. (*1 and 2 Thessalonians*, pp. 174-75)

Question 6. God's justice goes beyond punishing the wicked. His justice also provides relief for the righteous. "Paul looks to God to grant rest to the afflicted. This word [relief] is frequently used by the Apostle, and nearly always in contrast to affliction, as here. It denotes freedom from restraints and tension. The prospect of such relief given by God Himself is held out before the suffering Thessalonians as something which will strengthen their spirits in the trying times through which they are passing" (Morris, *First and Second Epistles*, p. 201).

Question 8. When Paul says that he wants the people to be worthy, he does not mean that God's kingdom is something they can earn. When God calls us, we are certainly not worthy. However, he does not want us to remain in that condition. Paul's hope is that once we have been called, we will live the rest of our lives in a manner that is worthy. To do this, we need God's power working in us.

Question 9. Leon Morris points out that

> the use of separate articles in the Greek before "them that know not God" and "them that obey not the gospel" is most naturally taken as pointing to two groups of people. . . . "Them that know not God" refers, of course, not to people who have never heard of the true God, but to those who are culpably ignorant. It is the sort of thing that Paul speaks of in Romans 1:28, where he refers to men who "refused to have God in their knowledge." The second clause is then a specific example of this, and the most heinous of all, for it involves the rejection of the revelation that God has given in His Son. The gospel is a message of good news, but it is also an invitation from the King of kings. Rejection of the gospel accordingly is disobedience to a royal invitation. (*First and Second Epistles*, p. 204)

Question 10. "Paul has given thanks for the spiritual progress of his readers despite their difficult situation and has assured them of a reversal in their condition at the coming of the Lord. But the fact of their past progress and the assurance of the righteous judgment of the Lord are not sufficient to guarantee that the readers will stand firm in their faith and share in the future blessings. Christian perseverance is a matter of continuing prayer and continuing faith. So Paul at last expresses how he prays that his readers will eventually reach the kingdom of God through continuing to show the evidences of a living faith" (Marshall, *1 and 2 Thessalonians*, p. 181).

Study 9. 2 Thessalonians 2. How Can I Be Sure of God's Power?

Purpose: To give group members the assurance that God can and will protect them through the horrors which are to come.

Question 3. John Stott writes:

> The day of the Lord cannot be here already, [Paul] says, because that day will not come until two other things have happened. A certain event must take place, and a certain person must appear. The event he calls "the rebellion" and the person "the man of lawlessness", the rebel. Although Paul does not call him the "Antichrist", this is evidently who he is. John writes of the expectation of his coming. He will be in the world before he emerges into public view. But only when the rebel is revealed will the rebellion break out. Paul had told them this, and more, about the man of lawlessness, when he was with them. He chides them for their forgetfulness. "Don't you remember that when I was with you I used to tell you these things?" (v. 5). The safeguard against deception and the remedy against false teaching were to hold on to the original teaching of the apostle. The Thessalonians must neither imagine that he had changed his mind, nor swallow ideas that were incompatible with what he had taught them, even if it was claimed that these ideas emanated from him. Loyalty to apostolic teaching, now permanently enshrined in the New Testament, is still the test of truth and the shield against error. (*Gospel and the End of Time*, p. 158)

Question 4. The "lawless one" is the same being that 1, 2 and 3 John refer to as the "antichrist" and Revelation 11:7 calls "the beast." The Bible prophesies that this individual will oppose God and claim to be in the place of God. *The New Bible Dictionary* explains: "Paul thinks of the supreme effort of Satan as not in the past, but in the future. He does not think of the world as gradually evolving into a perfect state, but of evil as continuing right up till the last time. Then evil will make its greatest challenge to good, and this challenge will be led by the mysterious figure who owes his power to Satan, and who is the instrument of Satan's culminating challenge to the things of God" (L. L.

Morris, in *The New Bible Dictionary*, ed. J. D. Douglas [Grand Rapids, Mich.: Eerdmans, 1962], p. 40).

Question 5. Many guesses have been made as to what is holding back the lawless one. Among the most widely held ideas are the Roman Empire, missionary preaching, the principle of order and God himself (perhaps through the person of the Holy Spirit).

> Paul is not describing some great series of events which take place in violation of the will of God, while He, so to speak, has to work out some plan as a counter. Paul thinks of God being in control of the whole process. While there are mysteries here, as there must be whenever we contemplate the workings of evil in a universe created by a God who is perfectly good, yet what is abundantly plain is that God is over all. No wicked person, be he Satan, be he the Man of Lawlessness, be he anyone else whatever, can overstep the bounds which God has appointed him. The Man of Lawlessness will be revealed only as and when God permits. He is not to be thought of as acting in complete independence. Throughout this whole passage, the thought of God's sovereignty is dominant. Evil is strong, and will wax stronger in the last times. But God's hand is in the process. Evil will not pass beyond its limits. God's purpose, not that of Satan or his henchmen, will finally be seen to have been effected. (Morris, *First and Second Epistles*, p. 227)

Question 6. Paul does not mean simply that evil is at work. That has always been true. He is talking here of a special form of evil which is hostile to all that Christ stands for. 1 John 4:3 is speaking of the same thing when it refers to "the spirit of the antichrist."

Question 7. According to Leon Morris:

> God is using the very evil that men and Satan produce for the working out of his purpose. They think that they are acting in defiance of Him. But in the end they find that those very acts in which they expressed their defiance were the vehicle of their punishment. Paul has the same truth in other places. For example, in Rom. 1:26 God gave up certain sinners 'unto vile passions.' They thought that they were enjoying their sinful pleasures. They turned out to be 'receiving in themselves that recompense of their error which was due.' The same truth is found in other parts of the Bible also. God is sovereign. No forces of evil, not Satan himself, nor his Man of Lawlessness can resist His might. He chooses to use men's sin as the way in which he works out their punishment. (*First and Second Epistles*, p. 234)

Question 9. God will spare us through our total dedication to the truth. Verse 10 says that it is those who refuse to love the truth that will be fooled. Verse 12 says that those who don't believe the truth will be condemned. Verse

13 says that the Thessalonian Christians will be spared because they have believed the truth. The truth which Paul refers to is the teaching of the early church which is now contained in the Bible.

Question 10. "The apostle's exhortation is a double one: 'Stand firm!' and 'hold to!' He seems to picture a gale, in which they are in danger both of being swept off their feet and of being wrenched from their handhold. In face of this hurricane-force wind, he urges them to stand their ground, planting their feet firmly on *terra firma*, and to cling on to something solid and secure, clutching hold of it for dear life. Both verbs are present imperatives. Since the storm may rage for a long time, they must keep standing firm and keep on holding fast" (Stott, *Gospel and the End of Time*, pp. 177-78).

Study 10. 2 Thessalonians 3. How Can I Be Sure That I Am Doing My Part?

Purpose: To help group members see the negative effects that laziness can have on a Christian community and to encourage them to take on their share of the load.

Question 1. Certain members of the church had apparently quit working and were now relying on the generosity of others for support. It is speculated that the reason for doing this was the expectation that Christ would soon return, making it pointless to prepare for the future here on earth.

Question 2. Paul includes the Thessalonians as his partners in spreading the message of Christ. Each of them is to join Paul in the fight against wickedness by praying and doing what he asks of them. Paul's statement in verse 4 that he expects them to "continue to do the things we command," is a set up for his command in verse 6. Thus, we can say that Paul expects each person to pray for the success of the gospel, obey the gospel and work hard.

Question 3. Leon Morris contributes the following:

> Paul was a very great apostle. But his greatness consisted not so much in sheer native ability (though he had his share of that) as in his recognition of his dependence on God. It arises out of this that he so often requests the prayers of those to whom he ministers. He did not feel himself as high above them, but as one with them. He valued their intercessions and sought their prayers. . . . He puts his imperative "pray" in an emphatic position, which leaves no doubt as to the importance he attaches to it, and he puts it in the present continuous tense, so that it means "pray continually." He looks not for a perfunctory petition, but for continuing, prevailing prayer. (*First and Second Epistles*, p. 244)

Question 5. The laziness of some was forcing the rest of the church to work harder in order to take care of the needs of those who would not work. It also may have given the church a bad reputation in the community. Paul also says that the idlers had become busybodies. Since they had nothing better to do, they spent their time spreading rumors and upsetting people.

Question 7. The idea of sacrifice is important to this question. Although by rights Paul did not have to work two jobs, he did in order to avoid every appearance of freeloading on others. He was willing to give up what was rightfully his in order to earn the right to preach the gospel.

Question 9. The lack of association included the avoidance of common meals, private hospitality in homes and other occasions where these idlers could continue to sponge off the other members. This was not to be used, however, as a means of expressing personal feelings of enmity. The offender was to still be loved and regarded as a brother or sister. The goal was not to chase people off, but to warn them and bring them back.

Question 10. "[Paul] is eager to protect the brother's standing, and to see to it that what is done to him is from the best of motives, and that it secures the desired results. The enforcement of discipline is a difficult matter. It is easy for men to become censorious and unnecessarily harsh in the process. Paul's words are directed against any such eventuality They are to be far from treating the offender as an enemy [There is to be] a steady refusal to have any truck with the evil thing, and a genuine concern for the well-being of the wrongdoer" (Morris, *First and Second Epistles*, p. 259).

Question 11. Your answer might include the following principles: (1) Discipline should not be given for a trivial offence, but only when God's word is deliberately and persistently disobeyed. (2) Discipline is to be given in the form of some degree of social ostracism from the rest of the church. (3) The responsibility for administering discipline belongs to the entire congregation. (4) Discipline should be administered gently and lovingly. The offender should not be treated as an enemy. (5) The purpose of discipline is not to humiliate, but to bring to repentance and reinstatement.

Donald Baker is pastor of First Reformed Church of Doon, Iowa, and Bethel Reformed Church of Lester, Iowa. He formerly served as a staff member with InterVarsity Christian Fellowship and is the author of the LifeBuilder Bible Studies Philippians, Judges *and* Decisions.